A Time for Everything

Julie Graham-Tremillo

Dedication:

I dedicate this book to my family, who have been extremely supportive in all of my endeavors; my husband, Antonio Tremillo, for his love and undying faith in me, my babies, Maya and Tomas for being the light that shines in my life, and my oldest daughters, Beth, Tushi, Cory, and Tara, who have been my best friends and have taught me so much.

Special thanks to my sisters, Tammy and Rosa for their encouragement and editing skills.

And of course to my Dad, Robert Graham, who taught me how to dream, and my Mom, Vivian Bell, who taught me how to be practical.

Table of Contents

Introduction:

Do you ever feel like you are being pulled in 15 different directions? On any given day, are there at least a dozen "minor emergencies" to deal with? Do you feel like if you take the day off, the whole world will grind to a halt because you didn't do something? If so, you are probably experiencing something we like to call "motherhood."

Motherhood is the most awesome job in the world. We work 24/7 with no pay. We are rewarded in hugs, kisses and cuddles when they are babies, and when they are older, we are rewarded with the best friends a person could ever have.

This job is not for the faint of heart. It will tax you to the very limit of your endurance, and when you don't think you can take anymore, it will push you even further. Luckily by the time it gets to that point, they are normally teenagers, so we have a few years of practice on us.

Things were different back in the day....my grandmother's time when moms always stayed home with the kids. They raised their food in the garden and the chickens in the yard. Fresh baked bread came from the oven, not the deli. Everything was made from scratch and nobody ever heard of instant mashed potatoes.

Times have changed, but we are no less "motherly." We still want good food on the table every night, a clean house and quality time with our kids. We just don't have as many hours in the day to do it because most of us have jobs where we spend 8 hours a day. Therefore, we can't spend 3 hours day baking bread, two hours in the garden, an hour feeding the animals, and another couple of hours doing the laundry on a washboard and hanging on the line. As much as we would genuinely love being able to do that...or not.

Luckily, we do have the corner deli for the fresh baked bread, and we can pick up the fried chicken in a box on the way home from work. With a little planning, you can have a meal on the table every night in about half an hour. More on that later....see our "Dinner Book" section.

There's more to life than just going to work and getting supper on the table, though. What about the 13 other things that are vying for your time every day?

My goal with this book is to show you how you can get more done with your time. You may not be less busy, but you should be less stressed out and you should be able to get more of the important things done.

Chapter 1 Take Smaller Steps and Maintain What You've Already Done

I am a busy person. I have tons of stuff to do every single day. If I get sick, in my mind, everything just kind of shuts down and I have to spend a week or so catching up. I am sure those around me only see a few extra toys laying on the floor or everyone having to eat pizza for dinner, but in my mind, everything has fallen apart.

I have six kids and I run my own business. It's pretty laid back now, because only four of my kids are at home and I am no longer going to college. At one time, I worked at a regular job for ten hours a day while I was going to college online and starting my business on the side, as well as taking care of those six kids who all lived at home at the time. No wait, scratch that, only five of those kids were at home...I was pregnant with the sixth.

As you can probably understand, I had to learn early to manage my time well. Not only did I have to learn to "manage my time"...I had to learn to MICRO-MANAGE my time. The more you can micro-manage, the more you can do. And I had ALOT that I needed to do.

Before I learned to micro-manage, my bathroom got cleaned when I noticed it was dirty and had time to clean it. The carpets and the floors got cleaned when I had a day off or when I couldn't stand it anymore. I dusted about once a year. While I did WASH clothes every day, they only got FOLDED about once a week.

The first thing that I learned to do was to take everything in smaller steps. You don't have to do it all at once. You can just do a little at a time. Chip away at the problem until it's gone, a little at a time. Deal with the new stuff as it comes in and chip at the old stuff. For example, I didn't have to fold five loads of clothes at once. I could just fold one basketful of clothes and then take a five minute break. What works for me is to set a time limit. For example, I am going to fold as many clothes as I can in ten minutes, and then I am going to put it away and go do something else. I was so surprised to learn what could be done in ten minutes. Something about setting that time limit made me work faster. I had to hurry and get it done.

Just as a quick side note to that "hurrying and getting it done" thing...when I do something really fast, I noticed that my heart rate would increase, which would increase my energy...something to do with adrenalin I am sure.

Another thing that I learned, which was difficult for me before, is that when you get something cleaned up, you have to keep working on it to get it to stay that way. You can't just clean something and expect that it is going to be clean for the rest of your life. If you clean off your dresser, you have to check back on it every day and make sure that it is still clean. Take a wash cloth and wipe it off. If you wipe it off, it forces you to check to see if little things are on there that shouldn't be there, like screws or little pieces of paper. You have to MAINTAIN what you have already done; otherwise you have to start over from the beginning.

Stuff attracts other stuff, junk attracts junk, dirt attracts dirt. If I lay an envelope on my dresser, the next day, it will have a couple more envelopes on top of it, and the day after that, it will have another envelope and a piece of paper and maybe a newspaper flier, and the day after that, it's going to have some of the kids legos or beads mixed in with it and my husband's screwdriver and my keys, and before you know it, I have this huge pile of junk on top of my dresser and it takes me weeks to get around to cleaning it again because it will take too long. So how to avoid that? DON'T PUT THAT FREAKIN ENVELOPE ON THE DRESSER!!!

Chapter 2 Where to Start

Does this sound familiar? It's 9:00 at night, just barely finishing supper, kids still have homework, nobody has taken a bath, the house is trashed, dishes all over the place, and everyone in the household is stressed out. The TV is probably blaring in the background distracting everyone. Laundry is piled up in the laundry room. You will probably have to do laundry tonight so the kids have clothes to wear tomorrow. At the very least, you will have to dig through that pile of clean laundry in order to find a matching pair of socks for tomorrow. Or worse yet, you wait until morning to find out you have to dig through that pile of laundry for socks.

You want to be a good parent, but you don't feel like a good parent because of the disorder in your house. You have physical disorder....the piles of dishes, laundry, and junk, and your family has mental disorder...stress, confusion, lack of schedules.

We have to fix that disorder. I'm going to help you. We are going to take one step at a time, put one foot in front of the other. We will break it down and micro-manage your time. By doing this, we will get everything done on your list of "things to do".

The very first thing I want you to do is to go lay out your clothes for tomorrow. Yours and your kids. Go ahead, go do that right now. I will wait for you. While you are laying out everyone's clothes, take note of whether or not they have clothes in their drawers for the next day. How hard is it for them to find their clothes for the next day? Are the socks sorted? Can you find socks? If you have no socks sorted, go ahead and match up two pairs of socks for each person, one for tomorrow and one for the next day. Go ahead and throw on a load of laundry while you are at it, you know you need to. I will be right HERE when you get back.

Ok, did you go lay out your clothes? Did you lay out your kids clothes? Did you sort two pairs of socks for each person and throw on a load of laundry? If not, stop right here and go do that. You won't get anywhere if you are skipping steps.

Chapter 3 Schedules are our Friends

Ok, so now that you have your clothes laid out, we can plan what comes next. Your day needs to be broken down into four blocks. The first block is sleep. That's the most important part. If you don't get that part right, it affects all the other parts. Don't neglect your sleep. Not always realistic, especially if you have babies that keep you up all night. Sleep when you can. Even ten minutes will help.

That being said, I know from experience that you can go for months or even years without a full 8 hours of sleep every night. Not recommended of course because your body will wear out. You will feel yourself getting older. So even if you can make it on less than 8 hours of sleep, try to avoid intentionally doing that. The second block of your day is the morning, which means from the time you get up until you go to work, however long that is. If you don't work, this block lasts until just before noon. You can probably get more done during this block of time than you realize. The key here is to be aware and to be active. Open your eyes look around. It's so easy to close your eyes and not see what's going on around you. STOP BLOCKING IT OUT!!! YOU HAVE A MESS, CLEAN IT UP!!!!

Your third block of time is the time that you are at work. And the fourth block of time is the evening after you get off of work.

Here is a typical morning for me: Alarm goes off at six and I hit the snooze until 6:25 (I have to do this to feel like I slept in). Get up at 6:25, immediately put on the clothes that I laid out the night before. Wake up the kids and have them go to the restroom. While they are doing that, make coffee and toast. Ask the kids what they want for breakfast (normally toast or cereal). Make their breakfast, sit down and eat with them until 7:00. My husband eats with us and he speaks Spanish, so we use this time to teach the kids a couple of words a day in Spanish. By 7:00 my caffeine is kicking in and the kids are done with breakfast, so I send them to get dressed into the clothes that they laid out (or I lay out) the night before. While they are getting dressed, I make my bed and put on a load of laundry. I also take a load out of the dryer and start folding it on my bed.

I then help them finish getting dressed and take them to school by 7:30. I get back home at 7:45. I don't have to work until ten, so I am lucky to have a couple of hours to work with here. Those of you who have to work earlier can move these things to immediately after work.

Depending on your personality, it may actually help you to write things on your schedule that will easily be marked off. For example, you might write "get out of bed," or "brush your teeth." By writing things that we know we will do, we have something to mark off as soon as we pick up our schedules. On the other hand, if you have too many things on your list, you might get overwhelmed before you get started. So as your list progresses and you develop your habits, you may be able to leave off some of the more obvious steps (such as getting out of bed).

Here is a sample of my schedule:

Morning schedule:
Get up 6:25
Get dressed
Wake up kids for school
Put on coffee
Put bread in toaster
Feed kids breakfast
Drink coffee, eat breakfast with kids
Make bed
Get kids dressed for school/fix their hair/check their backpacks
Brush teeth and fix hair
Take kids to school
Come home, fix makeup
Clean bathroom sink
Brush toilet

Wipe out tub
Wipe bathroom floor
Pick up dirty clothes
Put on a load of laundry
Fold a load of laundry or fold for ten minutes
and put away
Straighten bedroom and furniture
Make kids beds/straighten their room (ten
minutes or less only)
Wipe off countertops in kitchen
Check what's for dinner and thaw or put in
crock pot
Pick up and put away clutter
Have a cup of coffee or water, morning
meditation, refocus
Check calendar, lists, and weekly schedule
Do whatever is on the weekly schedule for today
Check problem areas (see list of problem areas)
Spend a few minutes on current "project"
Take vitamins
Check garden/plants
Go to work

Evening Schedule:
Come home and immediately start supper
Eat with family
Help kids with homework
Make sure kitchen is clean
Dry countertops and sinks
Put away papers/pick up and put away items in
living room

Sweep floors/wipe up spots
Wipe down kitchen floor
Clean off dining room table
Fold laundry/put away clothes/lay out clothes
for tomorrow including socks and shoes
Give kids a bath/brush their hair/make sure
they brush their teeth
Brush teeth
Take a bath
Use facial scrub or moisturizer
Get kids to bed by 9:00
Enjoy downtime
Go to bed at a decent hour

Some things need to be daily, some weekly, some monthly. So we try to set up our schedules to include everything that has to be done on a regular basis. Our daily schedules are broken down into morning and evening. Then we have our weekly schedules and then our monthly schedules.

Weekly Schedule:

Monday: vacuum, go through papers and bills, make lists, plan next week, make menus and grocery list for next week, bleach kitchen sinks and countertops, sweep floors

Tuesday: dust, clean refrigerator, clean microwave, sweep floors

Wednesday: do grocery shopping, clean stove, go to bank, pick up sticks and toys in yard, sweep floors

Thursday: clean out car, get gas, check fluids in car, clean kids bathroom, sweep floors

Friday: clean out purse and take coins out of purse, empty trash, shine mirrors, wipe door knobs, sweep floors

Saturday and Sunday: enjoy time with your family; change sheets

Monthly Project Areas:

Week One: living room/den, front entry way

Week Two: kitchen, dining room

Week Three: master bedroom, closet, laundry room

Week Four: kids' room, both bathrooms

Week Five: front porch, back porch, carport, other outside areas

Note: Week five is mostly outside. If for some reason, you cannot clean outside during week five (such as it is raining or cold the whole entire time), switch the work with week one for this month. So you would do the next week's work this week and do this week's work next week. I say this just because I know that I would try to skip week five when the weather wasn't perfect. Stop making excuses.

There are five weeks listed even though every month does not have a full five weeks. Week one and week five are normally partial weeks, which is why we put the lighter chores on those weeks. It will help if you get a calendar that you can mark on and go through the month and write in what you are working on during each week. Do this several months in advance. Use pencil in case you decide to rearrange your schedule. I like to keep my calendar in my kitchen on my refrigerator, right next to my daily, weekly and monthly lists. If you don't like keeping things on your refrigerator, you might consider getting a peg board or a magnetic board. I don't like dry erase boards for this because they are not permanent enough. My youngest daughter, though, has a dry erase board that is also magnetic and she keeps her schedule on that.

Chapter 4 Start Making Your Schedules

Before I learned to micro-manage my time, I saved all of my cleaning for Saturday and Sunday. Then I couldn't do anything on the weekend because I was cleaning. And if I did do something else on the weekend, the house didn't get cleaned and then everyone was stressed out. Now I keep my weekends free and only do my morning and evening schedules on the weekends.

I find that if I do everything on my list on the days that I am supposed to, eventually, it became habit and I don't even think about it. I automatically go shopping on Wednesday because that is when I am out of stuff anyway. There is a reason for each day. It's not really random. I put gas in the car on Thursday in case I want to go somewhere over the weekend. I clean out the refrigerator on Tuesday because I know I am going to the store on Wednesday. Keep in mind that you still have to be flexible. Maybe you go to the store on Tuesday night instead of Wednesday morning. Almost all of my weekly habits are done in the mornings. If there is something that I really don't like doing, I do that especially fast, so I get done with it. Don't be sloppy about it. You have to do it right, otherwise you have to redo it and that's even worse.

Start making your own schedules or print out a schedule from here if you are online. Build upon your list, just a little at a time. You don't have to do it all at once. Develop just a few habits at a time. If you print out the list and try to do each one, in order, it might take you some time at first. You have to keep stopping to see what is on the list next. That's fine to begin with. Eventually, you will memorize the list and you will do it all without ever looking at the list. Try to remember what is on the list next as you are working. Do that, and then check back with your list to make sure you have everything done. With my morning habits, I do about the first ten without ever thinking about what I am doing. Out of the whole list, there are only about two things that don't just come naturally to me yet, but they will. You have to customize the list. Just use mine as a guideline and make it fit your life. When you are making your list, put everything in the order that you would naturally do it in, so that you remember it more easily. For example, maybe you naturally do everything from left to right. If so, put it in that order. Whatever order you put your list in, try to do it in the same order every time, that way you make a habit of it and you do it naturally. If you find that you naturally do it in a different order, just change the order. When I first started trying to do my weekly habits, I tried to put my grocery shopping on Monday. After a few weeks I realized that I naturally do my grocery shopping on Wednesday. So I moved it to that day. I'm not saying I can't go to the grocery store on another day. But if you know you are going on Wednesday anyway, you might be able to just put what you need on the list and wait a day or two. And if you have to run to the store on the weekend for milk, try to pick up the rest of the things that are already on your list. That list, by the way, should be on a little pad on your refrigerator with a pen hanging beside it on a string. Sounds obvious, but it took me a while to figure out that a list on the refrigerator is easier to find than a list on your desk or in your notebook somewhere with all those other papers.

Chapter 5   Find a Focal Point

Find your focal point. The one area that has to be clean in order for you to feel like your house is clean. Mine is my bathroom, especially the sink, but really the whole thing. You can have more than one focal point. It is also a good idea to find your spouse's focal point. For my husband, it's the bed. Ha Ha, that sounds bad. No really, you can't just pull the covers up and think you are done. Everything has to be completely pulled off and remade every day, with the covers just so and the pillows exactly in place. It sounds kind of obsessive...and it is...but that's ok. Because when the bed is made just right, he feels like the rest of the house is clean, whether it is or not. It relaxes him, makes him calm, and makes him want to hang out. That's great because he is a workaholic and we have to convince him to relax.

Chapter 6 Evaluate your home

You have to evaluate your home before you can really get a handle on it. Take a clean spiral notebook (or just a piece of paper), walk through your house, being completely honest with yourself, and write down what you need to work on.

What are your problem areas? Is there a perpetual pile of clothes on the chair in your bedroom? Clutter on top of your dresser, a pile of dishes in the kitchen that never seems to get put away? Write down each of those things. Go room by room and write down everything. Make special notes of the perpetual problem areas. Those will be the ones that you need to keep an eye on and maintain regularly. You have made a habit out of allowing that area to become cluttered, so now you have to break that habit.

When you get to your kids' room...shut the door and walk away. Ha Ha, just kidding. No really, though, I know that's probably the worst room in your house, unless your kid is just obsessively neat, in which case, you are incredibly blessed. For the rest of us...in your kids' room, your first focus will be to clear a walkway. So write that on your list.

In each room that you walk into, stand in the doorway and look at the room. Where is the first place your eyes go? If it's a pile of clutter, that needs to go on your list. Make sure to clear every area that you can see from the doorway. Analyze each room and see if there is a way to re-arrange it so that areas that are bound to get messy are not directly in your line of site. For example, in your kids room, if the first thing that you see is a bookshelf, you may want to move that bookshelf to a wall that faces away from the door, or put a chair in front of it to block it from the door. I know it sounds like you are just hiding the mess when you do this. In a way, you are. You know that bookshelf is the messiest area of your kids' room. When you go in and organize the books, it looks really nice. You like to look at it…right up until your kids go and shove ten books into it sideways and then stuff their papers on top of that. So straighten it up, and then either move it or put something in front of it to make it where it is not as obvious. A desk is another area that is inclined to do this. A desk can look really nice and neat, until your kids do their homework. So you might consider moving that out of your line of vision. Instead, find something to put in your line of vision that is big enough to always look like it is clean. A large piece of furniture works well for this, such as a bed or a television. When I open my bedroom door, the first thing I see is the bed. It is always kept made, so the room looks clean. Before I rearranged my room, when I opened the door, the first thing I saw was the top of my husband's dresser. That is one of the hardest areas to keep clean, because as soon as I clear it, he will come in and empty his pocket onto the dresser. That's the funny thing about men; they store all of their "stuff" on their bodies. Women have purses for that. Men have stuff in every pocket.

So anyway, that dresser used to be right in my line of vision every time I opened the bedroom door, which was fine when it was clean. So instead of stressing out about keeping that dresser cleared constantly, I moved the dresser out of my line of vision. So check every room and see if you can rearrange it so that problem areas are out of your line of vision. I'm not saying that you should not work on those areas. Keep working on them, but you don't have to see that area every time you open the door. They are a work in progress. Every time you see clutter, instead of thinking of it as some big area that you will eventually get to, you should think of it as a work in progress. By definition, that means that you are working on it. So start working on it. Walk over to it, pick up one item that does not belong there, and go put it away. Ok, now it is a work in progress. Do that every day.

Chapter 7 Laundry

Laundry is one of those things that get out of control fast. You have to work on it daily to keep it under control. The great thing is, you have two machines helping you out. Ok, I realize that some people have to go to the Laundromat, so you can't do laundry daily. In that case, you will have to set aside time one day a week to do your laundry. But when you bring it home, fold it all and put it away immediately, don't just throw it in the corner.

For those of you who are lucky enough to have a washer and dryer, count your blessings. You know when you pick up your dirty clothes and put them in the laundry? That's when you put on a load to wash. You are in the room anyway, you might as well save yourself a few steps and start a load. I am a firm believer in doing what comes naturally. So if you are in the bathroom, you wipe down the sink, in the kitchen, you wipe off the counter, in the laundry room, put on a load of laundry. When you leave each room, you are leaving with something accomplished, instead of having to go back to that room later to do the exact same thing.

I use a big round tote for my clean laundry. Some would say to use a smaller basket so that you fold more often. I tried that. It doesn't work for me. As soon as I wash one blanket, my basket would be overflowing and I would feel like I was behind. If you let yourself, you will always feel like you are behind. Don't let yourself think like that. Move forward, but don't try to "catch up." Remember, it is a WORK IN PROGRESS.

I fold laundry every morning. I am going to let you in on a BIG SECRET that took me literally twenty years to figure out. This is HUGE and LIFE ALTERING, so pay attention. You know all those mismatched socks? And you know how the pile seems to grow every time you do laundry? Well mine did anyway. Well listen, because this is apparently a closely guarded secret...DUMP THE BASKET OUT BEFORE YOU START FOLDING. That's it. That's the secret.

You see, I used to leave everything in the basket. I would fold all of the clothes, but the socks would all sift to the bottom of the basket. So each time I did laundry, there was a bigger pile of mismatched socks. I would get to that part and then something in my brain would tell me that I was done, so I would stop. Every few weeks I would have to sit down for an hour or so and sort socks. So finally, after twenty years, I decided to dump the basket. This amazing thing happened. Even though the socks were still mostly saved for last, my brain didn't say, "I'm finished." My brain saw socks all spread out just begging to be mated because I could then SEE THE MATES more easily than if they were piled on top of each other in the basket.

This may not seem like a big deal to most people, but when you fight with sorting socks for eight people for 20 years, you appreciate these kinds of things. Such a simple, seemingly obvious thing that was NOT OBVIOUS to me at all.

Also, there is no reason why you can't make your laundry room a fun place to be. I would be willing to bet that you spend more time in there than anyone else. Therefore, you should be able to make it as pretty and as girly as you want without anyone complaining about it. Look around. Start with getting it organized the way you want it. Maybe an extra shelf or two. Maybe a fold down table that you can fold your clothes on as they come out of the dryer. Then decorate. Get bright colored curtains or paint the room a bright color. Most laundry rooms are really small, so if you paint them a dark color, it makes it look like a cave. But choose a color that makes you happy and makes you feel good when you walk into the room. I like a sunny yellow or a coral color for the laundry room. The sunlight from the tiny windows seems to bounce off of that color. If you can't paint it, find a way to let light in, whether it is lighter colored curtains, or better lighting. Make it a room you enjoy being in.

Chapter 8 Kids' Room

My kids' room is always the worst room in the house, even when it's "clean." The reason is obvious. They have so much "stuff." Clothes and shoes and toys and books. And when they start school, they have all these papers that are sent home, every single day. So those papers get shoved in with all the toys and other stuff. Even when it's clean, it's like one big disaster area just waiting to happen.

Another thing that adds to this mess is that your kids probably don't know how to clean it. It is overwhelming to them. It's probably overwhelming to you. Remember how when you were little, the hallways in your school seemed so big. Then when you went back years later, they seemed much smaller? Well, it's like that with the mess in their room. So if it seems like a big mess to you, it probably seems like a mountain to them. So your job is to make it less overwhelming. Be sure and praise their efforts and work with them. Try not to redo what they have done, even if it's not perfect. And it won't be perfect. But if you redo what they have done, they will feel like you don't approve and that they aren't good enough. Instead of encouraging them to do better, it will make them give up. So don't do that to your kids. Praise their work. No matter what it is. Praise it. Clean their room with them until they get it under control. If you don't like the way they make their bed, then next time, you make their bed while they pick up their toys. But don't make it seem like you are doing it because they did it wrong. You just do it different than they do. No matter what, don't make them feel bad about their efforts. As long as they are making the effort, that's all that matters. Encourage them to personalize their bed, add toys to it and pillows, and decorate it. LET THEM DO THIS. It's their bed; it should have on it what comforts them. You just need to make sure the covers are on straight.

Everything in their bedroom (and in the whole house) should have a home. If it doesn't have a home, find one. How can they clean their room if there is no certain place to put everything? I love shelving and drawers and hooks and pegs and anything else that helps you organize. But you have to USE these tools.

In this ONE ROOM ONLY you are allowed to be more lenient with your organizing. Go for more general ideas. For example, all games go into one bucket. All doll clothes can go together; you don't have to separate the baby doll clothes from the Barbie doll clothes. Use your own judgment on this and try to group toys together that they play with together.

It's so easy to try to micro-manage every detail here. But these are kids. The more detailed you make the sorting, the harder it is for them and the less likely it is that they will do it.

Finally, make them a list and post it in their room. Make it fun. Use pictures. But keep it simple. Post their morning schedule and their after school/before bed schedule. Don't put too many things on this list, especially at first. It takes time to develop a habit. Just because you are all excited about getting your house in order doesn't mean that your kids are excited about it. So give them one or two things at a time, such as "lay out your clothes for tomorrow," and "make your bed" (mornings). Add a few things that they already do, like "brush your teeth," and "take a bath." Hopefully they already do those things. If not, the sooner they learn, the better (even more important than making their beds...I am sure you agree). But if they already do those things, adding them to the list will give them something that they can mark off automatically, which will give them a sense of accomplishment. Once you get their lists made, put them in a plastic sheet protector, or laminate it if you have the capability. The sheet protector or laminate will keep the list clean and unwrinkled and they can use a dry erase marker on it if they want to mark it off every day. My kids used to mark off everything, but they got tired of erasing it, so now they just look at the list and go do what is next.

Chapter 9 Bathroom

As I mentioned before, my bathroom is my focal point. As long as my bathroom is clean, I feel like my house is clean. I keep bleach in the little container that the toilet brush is kept in. I use that every morning and then wipe down the mirror with a cloth that is just damp on the corner. I then wipe down the sink with the same cloth, paying close attention to the area around the base of the faucet. I shine the faucet with a dry cloth to get the water spots off and then dry the sink so that it doesn't have water spots. Water spots make your sink get dirtier faster, and then you end up having to scrub it.

I wipe out the tub. It doesn't require much because I wipe it out at night after I take a bath. Last, I take the wash cloth and wipe the entire floor, all the way to the corners, working my way to the door.

The whole process takes less than five minutes every morning. Even if everything looks clean, I still do it. If I wait until it looks dirty, I have waited too long.

Chapter 10 Rhythm

When you practice your habits daily, you are doing these same habits over and over....eventually you will develop a kind of rhythm. Everything will flow. Your morning habits will naturally flow without you having to think too much about it.

Think of how you normally get your work done without your new habits. I know how it was for me. I would jump from one thing to the next and zigzag all over my house, wasting a lot of extra steps.

Think of how you shop. Do you zigzag all over the store from one end to the other? Or do you start on one side and work your way to the other, picking up everything you need along the way? Hopefully you don't zigzag. As much fun as that is, it's not very functional and it will take longer. We are all about functionality, efficiency, and streamlining.

So when you are doing your morning habits, DON'T ZIGZAG. Find your rhythm. Start at one point and work your way to the other. Example-walk into your room, make your bed, pick up all the dirty clothes in that room, and put them in the laundry room. While you are in there, start a load of laundry. Take any clean laundry out and place it on your folding station. Mine is my bed (which is already made). Dump out the basket. Fold the clothes and put them away. If you put away clothes in the kids' room, pick up a few things while you are in there. Don't get distracted, though. You still have to go put away the rest of those clothes. So, although you touch on the kids' room, you don't stay there.

You have wash cloths and towels to put away, so while you are in each bathroom, do a quick two minute clean up: wipe down the mirror, then the sink, then run the brush around your toilet and wipe off the rest of your toilet with toilet paper (you don't want to get your wash cloth that dirty). Wipe down the floors right quick with that wash cloth and pick up any dirty laundry, towels or wash cloths. Leave the bathroom and go back and finish putting away those clothes.

I know this seems like you are jumping around, but you are not, because you keep coming back to your central point, which is the laundry at that time.

Chapter 11 Hidden/Secret Garden

I like to have hidden areas of my house that have unexpected charm. Like when you walk around a corner and see something cute and go "oh, look at that, I didn't expect to see that there." Such as a window seat with books in it, or a statue in the bathroom. It doesn't have to be a large area, maybe just a plant in an unexpected place, like the laundry room. Stairs are especially fun for this. If you have stairs in your house, look around on the Internet for ideas of what can go around your stairs, such as book cases under them, or drawers, or a seating area. Look at the top of your stairs too and see if there may be enough space to put an alcove with seating. Kids especially love these little nooks. They enjoy the enclosed feelings. Maybe it gives you a place to just get away for a few minutes. If you really look around your home, you may be surprised at how many hidden areas you can find like this for window seats or shelving or drawers for extra storage. Think outside of the box.

I had some friends who went to a Bed and Breakfast. They posted pictures. It made me realize that I would like my house to look more like that. And there is no reason that it can't. LESS CLUTTER, MORE QUALITY! Instead of having fifteen pillows that I "kind of" like, I could have two or three pillows that I really love. Create your own luxury. Create your own bed and breakfast in your home, just for your family. Create your own peaceful get-away. Make your house the place that your family wants to be when they are not at work or school. Why should you have to go away on vacation to stay in a luxurious suite when you can create it in your own home? Don't jump in and start spending a lot of money on remodeling. Start small, getting rid of the junk, and slowly bringing in one thing at a time that you really love.

Chapter 12 Motivation

It's all about the attitude. You can't resent the fact that you are "the only one cleaning" (whether you actually are or not). You have to do the work because you want to do it.

There are two types of motivation, intrinsic and extrinsic. In a nutshell, intrinsic motivation is when you are motivated from within. It is also commonly referred to as "self-motivation." Extrinsic motivation is an external motivation, such as when you are motivated because someone pays you to do something or they reward you in some other way. This is a positive form of extrinsic motivation. Or you are motivated because someone yelled at you and told you to do it or you are otherwise punished for not doing it. This is negative form of extrinsic motivation. While positive extrinsic motivation is more effective than negative extrinsic motivation, the most powerful motivation is intrinsic.

You have to be intrinsically motivated to get your house (and your life) in order. Something within you has to make you decide to get your house in order. No amount of extrinsic motivation can make you do it for any length of time. Oh, it may work on a temporary basis. Your mother-in-law is coming to visit, so you are extrinsically motivated to clean your house. But that won't have a lasting effect. You have to get your house in order because of something within you, such as, it makes you feel good, it makes you feel at peace, and it makes you think you are a good parent. Whatever the reason, it has to come from within.

You have to decide that it is something that you want in order to have any kind of lasting results. Since intrinsic motivation is the only form of motivation that has any kind of lasting effect, you have to nurture the intrinsic motivation. You cannot teach intrinsic motivation, but you can nurture it.

Encourage your kids. Be positive. Tell them what a good job they are doing. And if they are NOT doing a good job, DO NOT yell at them. If you yell at them, the motivation once again flips to being extrinsic motivation. "I don't want to do wrong because I may get yelled at." You don't want your kids thinking like that.

Make sure your relationship with your kids is a positive relationship. They should feel comfortable coming to you with their problems and with their mistakes. If they are afraid of making mistakes, they aren't expanding their minds. You are forcing them to think inside of a box. They will be afraid to try new things. When they do something like make their bed or clean their room, or even draws a picture, DON'T focus on what they did wrong. There will always be something that you think is wrong because it is not done your way. Don't be a control freak. Let them figure it out on their own. Let them see your example. When they are being creative, encourage it. Don't tell them it's wrong. Art is never wrong. Creativity is never wrong.

Nurture the intrinsic motivation. "Wow, it's so great that you picked up your toys without being told." Let them know that it's ok to make mistakes. Your home should be a safe environment where it's ok to mess up. It should be peaceful and comfortable. It should be a safe haven, a sanctuary for them. Your kids should trust that you won't freak out on them. They should feel relaxed around you.

Another note about intrinsic motivation…. If someone is intrinsically motivated to do something (such as clean their room) and you try to give them extrinsic motivation (such as you try to pay them for it, or they leave one thing out of place, so you yell at them), the intrinsic motivation could die off. They will no longer be self-motivated to clean their room. You have to keep a positive attitude. If you are doing the work with a negative attitude, you will become resentful. When you do that, your family can feel it. You cannot create intrinsic motivation in them, by the very definition of intrinsic motivation, you cannot do it. All you can do is set an example, and hope that they follow it. So stop acting like a martyr. Do your work out of love for your family and don't act like you resent it or try to make them feel guilty about it.

I'm not saying you shouldn't give them age appropriate chores, but if they don't do it, don't freak out. Find them something else to do. Get their input. Do it calmly. I cannot stress enough the importance of not freaking out on your kids. The whole reason we want our houses clean is so that our families will have peace. If you are freaking out about it, you have defeated the purpose. We want to create a peaceful and stress-free environment for our families. It will take some time.

Be flexible, even though you micro-manage your time. Someone is GOING TO come along and mess up your schedule. IT WILL HAPPEN so be flexible and DON'T FREAK OUT ABOUT IT. Consider it part of your downtime. It's all about the attitude, all a matter of perspective.

Everyone needs downtime. Try to schedule downtime daily, like every night after 8:00. Do something that you enjoy, that helps you relax. Mine is reading. You need downtime so that you don't get burnt out.

Chapter 13 Feng Shui and Meditation

I like to dabble in a little bit of Feng Shui. Just a touch, mind you, I am not going into great detail. Feng Shui deals a lot with getting rid of clutter. When our houses are cluttered, our minds are also cluttered. When you look around your house and see piles of junk, it stresses you out, whether you realize it or not. When your house is neatly organized, clean and uncluttered, your mind is calm, relaxed. When your mind is calm and relaxed, you feel less stress. You can allow your mind to focus on other things, to be more creative. Allow your mind to see greater possibilities, relax and feel at peace in your house.

I have always felt that my home should be a "sanctuary" for my kids. It should be a place that they can go to feel safe and loved, and feel peace. If they feel safe and loved and at peace, they can learn and grow. They can become better people. They will learn to love and be at peace. It is important that we provide a peaceful environment for our kids.

I have also worked toward teaching my children basic meditation. This helps to calm them. My two youngest kids are 8 and 6 now. There are so many different forms of meditation. The type of meditation I use with my children is about finding inner peace, finding their "happy place." Teach your children to listen to sounds that calm them. I put a small table top waterfall that has a soft light, in their room. You can get them for about $20. I turn it on before they go to bed. They fall asleep listening to the sound of the waterfall. This is a form of meditation. They hear that same sound and it is soothing to them. They fall asleep peacefully. Don't let them fall asleep to the television. No telling what kind of dreams they will have, even if they are watching cartoons. This is one of those times when you can control what goes into your children's minds. Their minds are vulnerable as they are falling asleep. Make sure to put something good into it.

Chapter 14 Fitness

I am the world's laziest person when it comes to fitness. I always think that I don't have time for it. Shouldn't I be doing something more important? Isn't there something that needs cleaned or some kind of work that needs done? Well yes, there probably is. But you have to take care of yourself if you expect to be able to take care of others. I figured this out when I was dragging through every single day, barely making it, and then falling in bed exhausted, only to wake up almost as tired as before I went to bed and do it all over again.

I was eating right (sort of), got plenty of vitamins and protein, so I didn't understand why I had no energy. I kept hearing that if I exercised, I would have more energy. That didn't make a bit of sense to me. How was doing MORE stuff supposed to make me have more energy? But still, after years of being pushed into it, I gave it a try. Guess what? I actually did have more energy. And I slept better at night. So squeeze in a little time for exercise. You can do most of it while you are standing around in the kitchen. And if you have a little extra time, it's always more fun if you exercise with friends or family.

If you absolutely have no extra time at all, you don't have to just give up on exercise. Exercise can be incorporated into your everyday life. I am no expert on exercise (understatement of the year), and I am certainly no doctor (duh) so talk with your doctor if you have heart problems, etc. (my disclaimer). I think that everything that we do can be considered exercise, dependent on how we do it. If we are sluggish about our housework and take forever to do it, that probably couldn't be considered exercise. However, if we do it really fast and put as much motion into it as possible, move more, be more active. Maybe squat instead of bending. Look at everything you do and see how you can maybe put just a little exercise into it, just to make your muscles stretch a little or get your heart rate going. That's the big thing with me, getting my heart rate going. Once I get my heart rate going, I will have more energy and can do more things. I am also much less depressed when I am more active. Some people are just naturally happy people and I think that is awesome. I would love if I were like that. But I'm not, no matter how I try to fake it. I am naturally very subdued and tend to get depressed easily. I'm sure I could use some psychological help with that, but I also have this habit of trying to fix everything, so I work on myself.

The point is that exercising gives me more energy and more energy makes me less depressed and less stressed out. So I try to stay really active with everyday things.

Chapter 15 Vinegar diet

Years ago I ran across a "vinegar diet." The idea is to eat just a little bit of apple cider vinegar every day. It is supposed to speed up your metabolism. This should give you more energy. It is also supposed to help you lose weight (but only if you actually need to lose weight). I don't know how scientific it is. But I can say that it works for me. I notice when I have just a little vinegar every day, I have more energy and I don't feel like I am dragging through the day. I also seem more alert.

I've also known a few people who have tried it to lose weight and it worked for them.

As a warning, if you drink straight vinegar, you will feel like someone tried to poison you. I know because I tried it. Seriously, don't do that. I used to take an apple and put it in a juicer (minus the core) and add a couple of teaspoons of vinegar. Now, I just buy a jar of unsweetened apple sauce, dip out what I want and add a teaspoon or two.

There are tons of recipes on the Internet for vinegar, such as adding it to salads. I am more a ranch dressing kind of person, so I save the vinegar for my apple sauce.

Chapter 16 Finances

Finances are like house work. Before you can start to clean it up, you have to throw open the curtains and shed some light into the corners. Once you see the dirt, you can clean it up. You can keep the curtains closed so that you can't see the dirt, but it's still there. Open your eyes. Deal with the priorities first, housing, bills, food...you know, the essentials. But eventually, you will have to deal with the corners too.

I am a firm believer of having multiple sources of income. I am not saying that everyone needs two full time jobs. I am actually against that because you spend less time with your family. Sometimes it's necessary though, and only you know your circumstances.

I recommend that each adult have one full time job. Any teenagers over the age of 16 will hopefully have a job too. It's important to teach your kids to work, even if only part time on the weekend. By that age, they should be able to buy their own things, like their clothing. If teenagers can buy their own "stuff," you can save your money for the things you need, like paying the bills.

Back to "multiple sources of income," maybe you can have a full time job and then do something else on the side. Like selling things on online, for example. We have groups set up on a social network in our county and we buy and sell things on there. This is a great way to get rid of some of your clutter and make a little extra cash. Items bring more online, than at a yard sale. At a yard sale, you have to put the stuff in the yard and then wait for someone to come and purchase it. If you sell it on online, you can put the price on it that you want, and if you don't get the price, you can just wait until someone comes along that wants to pay that amount. You don't have the time limit of a yard sale.

You may not make much money at first. However, you are opening a door for money to start coming through. The hard part is getting the door open. After that, you just keep working at it and eventually, more money will start coming through that doorway that you created.

I remember the first five dollar sale that I made. I sold a computer mouse out of my home. I was so excited about selling that mouse that I told my whole family about it. They all thought I was crazy, of course, making a big deal out of selling one thing. But I figured, if I could sell one, I could sell more. So if I only sold one mouse a week for five dollars, I could make an extra $20 a month. That's not a lot, but I was making minimum wage at the time, so it's not bad. So I made a goal to do that. And then I made a goal to sell two mice per week (or other computer items). I decided I needed a little advertising, so I put up a few flyers around town. I also tinkered a little with fixing computers, so I advertised that a little too. I got a few customers, people who didn't mind taking a chance on someone new if they could get it done cheaper. Of course, it was all just a side job because I had bills to pay and kids to take care of. So if I could sell a couple of mice a week, and maybe fix one or two computers a month, I was happy with that.

A few months later, I had another crazy idea to talk to some of the local business owners and see if I could put up a shelf or two in their businesses and sell a few items off of them, maybe have a place where customers could drop off their computers instead of bringing them to my house.

As luck would have it, I ran into someone who was just about as crazy as I was. She said, "Well, instead of doing that, why don't you just buy this shop from us?" That was a huge leap for me. Looking back, I think I had more guts than brains.

Six years later, I still have my shop. It was kind of touch and go for the first year or so. I'm not rich and I'm sure I won't get rich anytime soon, but I manage to pay the bills.

The point is, I started out by selling one mouse. I made a goal to improve upon that a little at a time. I was VERY DETERMINED, and EXTREMELY MOTIVATED. Somebody told me once that you have to be "hungry enough" in order to be successful. I never was sure if she meant that figuratively or literally. Either way, I have always remembered that. If you are hungry enough, you won't be sitting there watching TV or lounging about. You will be up, working towards your goal. As soon as you start lounging about, that's when you are not hungry enough.

If you can just find one little things that you can sell, whether it is service or a product, you will have a starting point for a business that you can focus on and make grow. I read a book once where a lady sold love potions. She even admitted that it wasn't real, it was just for fun. She bought them wholesale and had her little website on the Internet where she sold them. It sounded crazy, but it worked. It had nothing to do with her personality, and everything to do with finding a product that people want and marketing it.

My dad always told me I could do anything that I set my mind to do. I really believe him. I am sure plenty of people have heard that. But did you really think about it? How do you "set your mind" to something? I think that means that if you think about it long enough and hard enough, and if you really focus on it and don't give up, you will figure out a way to do it.

Chapter 17 Dinner

What's for dinner? Does it seem like you hear that question every single day? Doesn't it seem like you would have an answer ready for it? After all, how many years have you been cooking dinner? I know for me, it has been every night for 20 years. But I still have difficulty with that question.

So finally, I sat down to try to figure out how to solve the problem. Surely I could figure out a little thing like what's for dinner, right?

The first step for me was to identify the problem. My problem was that I wouldn't get home until 6:30 at night. At that time, I would walk through the door and my teenagers would say, "Hey Mom, what's for dinner?" If you have teenagers, you know that logic does not work on the teenage mind. So explaining to them that they had been sitting there for at least three hours before I got home and asking why they hadn't started dinner would have no effect whatsoever on them. It doesn't even matter if they know how to cook. Not to mention that, whatever they decided to cook, you probably would not consider a "meal." Ramen noodles, for example, are not a "meal." So when your teenager says they will cook dinner and you end up with ramen noodles on the table and nothing else…well you should have known better. Macaroni and cheese or hot dogs are also not considered a meal, even though your kids think it's great.

So here, we have identified two problems. First, you don't have time to cook. Second, even if your kids did help cook, the food is not going to be up to your standard.

So let's deal with that first problem. You want something to cook that is ridiculously easy, yet doesn't taste ridiculously easy. If you want to spend hours cooking, you can do that on the weekend, just for the fun of it, if that's your thing. But first, you need food to get you through the week when you don't have any time. In fact, you barely have time to read this book, right? So the first step is to come up with a list of recipes that do not take long to cook. I'm going to say 30 minutes or less. Even then, though, if you have to run to the store to get the ingredients, it is no longer a quick recipe.

With just a small amount of planning, you can get this method set up where you can walk in the door at 6:30 and have a meal on the table for your family by 7. So first, you come up with your recipes, and then you STOCK YOUR KITCHEN. This sounds so obvious, but it's really not. I mean, sure, you have the basics in your kitchen, milk, bread, flour, sugar, etc. But do you really have everything you need? Check your freezer. Do you have ground beef, chicken, roast? That's great. But, you need to go one step further. You need to buy in quantities that are easy to cook. And I understand that it's cheaper to buy a whole chicken, rather than deboned chicken strips, or it's cheaper to buy a whole roast rather than precut pieces. However, if that roast sits in your freezer and gets freezer burn because you never had time to cook it, you are defeating the purpose. I'm not saying don't ever buy whole roasts again. But use those for meals where you don't have to cut them up. Put those in a crock pot and let them cook all day. Don't think you can pull a roast out of the freezer at 6:30 at night and have anything edible on the table before 9. It's a different way of cooking and it's not the way your grandmother or even your mother did it. But it's what works for you, because you are a busy woman, but you still want good tasting food on your table every night. So we are going to create a few recipes and then a grocery list to go with it. You will need to keep all of these ingredients on hand at all times; otherwise, these recipes won't be quick recipes. And you have to use the shortcuts; otherwise, your dinner is going to be ready at 9 instead of 7.

Also, you need to plan which recipes you will be cooking on what days. So when you walk into your kitchen, you know exactly what you are going to cook. You aren't going to go stand in front of the refrigerator and ask yourself what's for dinner. And when your kids ask you that question, you will have an answer every day. So at 6:30, you will walk into the kitchen, put on a pan of water to boil (if you need it and most times you will) and pull out your ingredients BEFORE you kick off your shoes and pour yourself a glass of ice tea.

I have a general meal plan for the week and I keep it posted on my refrigerator. It looks something like this:

General Menu:

Sunday: Chicken- chicken with rice, baked chicken, chicken pot pie

Monday: Italian- Spaghetti, pasta, ravioli, lasagna

Tuesday: Mexican-tacos, beans and rice, chicken tacos, fajitas

Wednesday: Soup or stew in crock pot; lentils; lentils with barley

Thursday: Fish; sushi; Asian food; Asian noodles; lo Mein; chicken tacos; fish sticks

Friday: Salad with meat like turkey ham; create salad bar with eggs, craisins, etc

Saturday: Beef; beef tips; roast; brisket; corned beef brisket

This is just a guideline for when I don't know what to cook. I can just cook something off of the list.
Here are some other quick meal ideas:

Meal number one:

Chicken Soup

half a pan of water
raw chicken strips
chicken/tomato bullion
salt
frozen, canned, or fresh miscellaneous vegetables such as tomatoes, carrots, zucchini, potatoes, green beans, corn, or any other vegetables that you like

Place chicken strips in boiling water. Add
bullion and salt. Add vegetables. Cook until
done.

grocery list for this recipe: raw chicken strips,
chicken/tomato bullion, frozen and canned
vegetables

Chicken soup....you can get as creative as you
want with this meal. I start with raw chicken
strips (not the kind that are breaded). The
precut chicken strips are a little more expensive,
but they really cut down on the time it takes to
prepare the food. Get a big pot like you would
use to make spaghetti and fill it half full with
water. This is the pot of water that you should
have put on to boil as soon as you stepped into
the kitchen. Open your chicken strips, rinse
them off and drop them in the water. Continue
boiling. I like to use powdered chicken bouillon
or powdered tomato/chicken bouillon a lot
when I cook. I use, although I am sure there are
other brands. This is something that you season
to taste. I would add a couple of tablespoons of
tomato/chicken bouillon and then sprinkle some
salt into the water. You want your chicken to
cook with the seasonings. Because it is chicken
strips, it will have less flavoring, so you have to
add it. Next, you add whatever vegetables that
you have. I normally have frozen tomatoes and
frozen zucchini in my freezer from my garden,
so I would add some of that. Typically I add a
few pieces of zucchini and about a half a quart of

tomatoes. If you don't have those, you can add canned stewed tomatoes and skip the zucchini. You can add fresh vegetables too, like potatoes or carrots or celery. But be sure and cut them small, so that they will cook faster. If you don't have time for fresh vegetables, add some frozen. I would add about a half a bag of mixed vegetables or a large can of mixed vegetables. And if you have frozen potatoes and carrots, that would make it easier as well. Just make sure you have plenty of vegetables in it. If you are not careful, your soup will be bland, so taste it once the chicken is fully cooked and add salt to taste. For those of you who are extra adventurous, you can add cubed cheese in your soup bowls once the food is being served. The soup will melt the cheese and give it a richer flavor.

Leftovers:

Just a quick note about leftovers: I LOVE leftovers. Leftovers mean that I have a fully cooked, good tasting meal, just ready to be heated up and put on the table. But of course, if it didn't taste good the first time, it will taste even worse the second time. If you don't have enough leftovers to make a whole meal, consider just reheating the leftovers and using those as side dishes for your main meal.

Meal Number Two:

Tacos:
I never really get tired of tacos because you can make them different every time. I normally use corn tortillas, but you can use flour or you can use the hard crunchy shell. With the corn tortillas, I just heat them up in the microwave for about a minute and a half for five tortillas. That softens them enough that you can make tacos with them. Of course, don't heat the tortillas up until everything else is ready, though. My basic tacos are just ground beef that is very highly seasoned. I like garlic and cumin on mine, as well as some tomato chicken bouillon powder. I use a LOT of cumin. I have to be able to smell the cumin before I am happy with it. Of course, you should season it to taste. Add the salt last, though because the bouillon will have some salt in it. Add all the other seasonings while the meat is cooking, don't wait until the meat is done. Once the meat is fully cooked, I normally add a can of plain pinto beans and cook it a little longer like that.
For toppings, I like shredded cheese, lettuce, tomatoes, onions, avocadoes, salsa, and sour cream. All of those are optional
Alternatives: you can use any kind of meat in tacos. Sometimes I buy fried chicken from the deli and tear it up and put it in tacos.

Meal Number Three:

Corned Beef hash and eggs:
This could have probably gone as an alternative to meal number two, but I use it so much, I made it a meal in itself. It's super easy and fast to make. All you have to do is open a can of corned beef hash, put it in a skillet and start frying it. Then add several eggs, however many you want. I normally add at least five eggs to one can of corned beef hash. I serve this with steamed corn tortillas, shredded Colby jack cheese, lettuce, tomatoes, onions, and salsa. As with any taco, you can put whatever vegetables you like on it. Sometimes I even add kale or fresh spinach.

Meal Number Four:
Fajitas:
No, fajitas are not the same as tacos. I have a trick to my fajitas that makes it super fast and easy. I buy my meat preseasoned and presliced from the Mexican meat market. I normally buy beef, taco, and chicken. The taco meat is beef, but it is cut smaller. Just put the meat in a frying pan, turn it on medium heat, and cover. While that starts cooking, slice bell peppers and onions into strips. Dump the peppers and onions on top of the meat and cover. You will need to occasionally stir so that the meat doesn't stick. Once everything is fully cooked, you are ready to eat. Serve the fajitas inside tortillas and add whatever fresh vegetables you like with it.

Meal Number Five:
Baked Potatoes:
I like to do these the day after I make fajitas, or even with the fajitas. Clean your potatoes, poke holes in them with a fork, and put them in the microwave for ten or twenty minutes until they are soft (depending on how big the potatoes are and how many are in the microwave). Heat up the rest of your fajita meat. Set out butter, shredded cheese, salt, sour cream, and the meat and potatoes. Let everyone make their own baked potatoes to their liking. I love baked potatoes with fajita meat, butter, and lots of cheese. Some people also use frozen broccoli and heat it in the microwave with butter and then top their potatoes with it.

Meal Number Six:
Salads: This is another meal I like to make the day after I make fajitas. Salads are one of those tricky things that can either be really bland or really good. For a basic salad, throw in lettuce, tomatoes, onions, and chunks of cheese. Serve avocadoes on the side because they tend to go bad faster than the rest of the salad. I also like to keep the meats separate and then let everyone add their own. Also, if you have young kids, you probably want to keep the onions separate. Place nacho chips on the table as well (separate, to keep them from getting soggy). So when you serve your salad you will place the chips on the bottom, add the basic salad, add the fajita meat, onions, and whatever dressing that you like. Alternative: if you do not have fajita meat, you can add shredded fried chicken, which can normally be picked up at your grocery deli. I also like chopped turkey ham in salad. Depending on your taste and your family's taste, you might want to also think about tuna or canned chicken. I prefer to serve all of the meats on the side, in case someone doesn't like something. Also, try different kinds of vegetables, such as fresh kale or spinach, or olives. Pretty much any fresh vegetable or cooked meat can go in a salad. You could also try canned beans, such as Ranch Style beans, black beans, or pinto beans.

Basic Salad:	Optional meats:
Other variations:	
Lettuce	fajita meat
canned beans, drained	
Tomatoes	cooked chicken
avocadoes	
Onions (on side)	tuna
nacho chips	
	turkey ham
cheese	
sour cream	
cilantro	

Meal Number Seven:
Spaghetti:
This is another meal that can be really good or really bland. First, put a pot of water on to boil. Get your ground beef started cooking. Hopefully it is thawed, if not, put it in the microwave for about 5 or ten minutes depending on how much it is. Don't let it overcook in the microwave or it will be bland. Season your water and your meat. For the meat, add tomato chicken bouillon powder, several tablespoons, cumin, oregano, and garlic. You can add salt later to taste. Don't add it yet, though because the bouillon has salt in it. Season the water for your pasta. Add garlic, salt and tomato chicken bouillon. Once the water is boiling, break the spaghetti in half and drop it into the water. Cook until it is al dente (firm, not crunchy, not soggy). Once the meat is fully cooked, add a couple of large cans of Hunt's Spaghetti sauce. I like the kind with garlic. Now here is my secret ingredient that not everyone will like, but my family won't spaghetti without it…Sugar. Add about a quarter cup of sugar to the spaghetti sauce. This will give it a slightly sweet taste. You can add a little more or a little less, depending on your taste. Add a little at a time until you like it. The sugar softens the taste of the spaghetti sauce so that it doesn't taste as acidic. Cook it for a little while so that the meat can soak up the flavoring from the sauce, about

10 to fifteen minutes on low heat, stirring occasionally. Drain the pasta, rinse with cold water, and drain again. Serve the pasta and sauce separately and let everyone dip their own sauce. Garlic toast is a good side dish for this. Just toast bread, spread butter on it, and sprinkle with garlic. I also like French bread with it and I put garlic and butter on that as well.

Meal Number Eight:
Chicken Pot Pie:
uncooked chicken strips
cream of chicken soup
frozen or canned mixed vegetables, drained
frozen deep dish pie crust (2 if you want a top crust)
seasonings to taste

Put water on to boil immediately. If chicken is still frozen, put it in the microwave for a few minutes. While chicken is thawing, add seasonings to your water. . I like powdered chicken bouillon or chicken tomato bouillon. Add raw chicken strips to water. Preheat oven to 350. Cook the chicken until it is completely done. Remove chicken from water; pour cream of chicken soup in microwave safe bowl. Add frozen mixed vegetables to the soup mixture. Heat soup and vegetable mixture in microwave until hot. Tear the chicken into small bite size pieces. Mix the chicken in with the soup and vegetable mixture. Poke holes in frozen pie crust with fork. Pour mixture into pie crust. At this point, you can either put it in the oven like this or you can add a top pie crust. For a top pie crust, I normally use another frozen pie crust and cut it in pieces and put it on top. You can try for a lattice look, but don't get picky with it, it's just supper, it's not like it's a beauty contest.

Meal Number Nine:
Beef stew: or any other kind of food that you can throw in a crock pot. It doesn't take long to throw everything together in the morning in a crock pot. Turn it on low and leave it cooking. When you get home, you have dinner waiting for you, almost as if someone else cooked it. Just throw any kind of meat into a crock pot, add an onion, and some carrots, maybe some potatoes, fill it almost to the top with water, add seasonings (tomato chicken bouillon), and then just let it cook.

Meal Number Ten:
Chicken or tuna fettuccine Alfredo: cooked chicken or tuna, Alfredo sauce from a jar (Prego has some good sauce), and any kind of pasta, including fettuccine.

Categorize your meals to make it easier. Have themes for each night. For example, Monday can be Italian night (spaghetti, fettuccine, ravioli, or lasagna); Tuesday can be Mexican food (tacos, fajitas, enchiladas, tamales); Wednesday can be American food (hamburgers, hot dogs, etc). By making a different theme for each day of the week, you can have a better idea of what you want to make for dinner each night. It's also a good idea to have "default meals." If for some reason you can't cook whatever you have on your menu (you are out of the ingredients, for example), you can fall back on a few default meals. A default meal is a meal that you always have the ingredients for. That is the meal that you make when you can't think of anything else. I have two default meals, tacos and spaghetti. I always keep all of the ingredients on hand for both meals.

It's a good idea to also have one or two quickie meals in mind and have the ingredients for that. A quickie meal is something that you can throw together when you have no time at all that will take less time than going out to eat fast food. Here are a few to give you an idea:

Sandwiches: any kind, as complicated as you want. Think of subway and how they have all of these options for sandwiches. Different breads, different meats, vegetables, cheeses, sauces. Just make sure that anything that you buy for your quickie meals gets used up before they go bad. Black beans and corn: This is one of my favorites and super easy. Take two cans of corn, two cans of black beans, open and drain all of them. Dump them into a microwavable bowl; add a large tablespoon full of margarine for flavoring, and a couple of handfuls of shredded cheddar or colby-jack cheese. Microwave until it is heated through and the cheese is melted. Serve it with chips or inside of soft, warm corn or flour tortillas. A side of lettuce is good with this and maybe some sour cream and salsa if you like spicy foods.

Frozen ravioli with Alfredo sauce: I love this for a really quick meal. You can either boil it or throw it in the microwave. It just takes about five minutes and will keep you from going down and blowing your money on fast food. Plus, I am lazy, so making a trip to Burger King takes too much energy when I can just pop this in the microwave. Add a small salad with it and you have a full meal. Maybe even some bread sticks if you feel so inclined.

Here is a list of basic foods you should always have on hand. Edit this to fit your needs.

Basic foods you should always have on hand:
milk
butter
eggs
bread
tortillas: corn and flour
cheese
cream cheese
sour cream
fresh vegetables: lettuce, tomatoes, onions, carrots, potatoes, avocadoes
salad stuff: bacon bits, craisins, croutons
salad dressings: ranch and Italian
condiments: mayonnaise, ketchup, mustard
frozen vegetables: mixed vegetables, broccoli, cauliflower
frozen meats: chicken leg quarters, boneless skinless chicken, roast, beef tips
dry beans
lentils
barley
rice
canned foods: pinto beans, black beans, corn, mixed vegetables, hominy, asparagus, green beans, red spaghetti sauce, alfredo sauce
frozen ravioli
frozen pie crust
dry pasta: spaghetti, elbow macaroni, fettuccine

flour

sugar

salt and other seasonings; cumin, powdered
tomato chicken bullion

drinks: tea, coffee, creamer, juice

breakfast: cereals, pancakes

canned meats: tuna, chicken, corned beef, corned
beef hash

nacho chips

nacho cheese

lunch meat and sandwich stuff

I know it seems like a lot of lists and organizing.
But don't start out with a full list. Start with just
a little at a time. Chip away at the problem.
Deal with new stuff as it comes in and chip away
at the old stuff. Develop just a few habits at a
time. This applies to your clutter, your finances,
any problem that you have. Rome was not built
in a day.

This is our journey where we seek peace, order,
and happiness for ourselves and our families.
We are all at different places in our journey.
Only YOU know where you are along that
journey. So evaluate yourself and your life.
Figure out where you are along your journey.
And then take your habits that you already have
in place and build around them.

Do this for yourself and your family. Even if
you live alone, you need to love yourself enough
that you give yourself this peaceful
environment. Make it a part of who you are, not
just something that you do.

Embrace the organization, the order, the
cleanliness and the peace. Do it because YOU
want to do it. It's all about the mindset.

Made in the USA
Charleston, SC
11 July 2013